In this book, we're going to talk about the country of Vietnam—its culture and geography as well as the 20-year war called the Vietnam War. So, let's get right to it!

Vietnam Market

STUCK IN VIETNAM

Culture Book for Kids
Children's Geography & Culture Books

BABY PROFESSOR
EDUCATION KIDS

Speedy Publishing LLC

40 E. Main St. #1156

Newark, DE 19711

www.speedypublishing.com

Copyright 2017

FACTS ABOUT VIETNAM

The country of Vietnam is on the continent of Asia. It's in a section of Southeast Asia that is a peninsula called Indochina. The official language spoken there is Vietnamese, but there are at least seven other languages spoken including French and Chinese.

The Vietnamese language is very difficult to learn since there are six different tones that change the meanings of words.

Most Vietnamese children study English as a second language in school.

Over 93 million people make Vietnam their home. Their government is a socialist republic, which means they are under communist rule. The landmass of the country is 127,123 square miles. The country's capital city is Hanoi. The flag of the country has an orange background with a yellow star at its center.

Can Cau Market

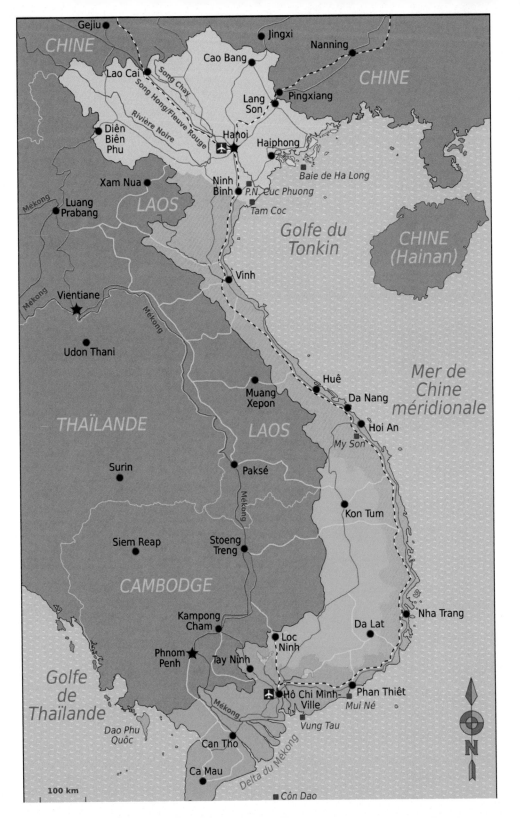

GEOGRAPHY OF VIETNAM

The country of Vietnam is a long skinny piece of land that is s-shaped. It is bordered by China to the north and Laos and Cambodia to the west. Its east coast is about a thousand miles long with the Gulf of Tonkin to the north and the South China Sea to the east and south. The beautiful Annam Cordillera mountains hug the western side of the country.

Vietnam is not very wide across. There are parts of the country that are only 30 miles wide. The country is traversed by four major rivers—the Mekong River, the Red River, the Ma River, and the Perfume River, which was named for the tropical scent that it used to bring down from the mountains.

Perfume River

Mekong River

The Mekong River, which is in the southern part of the country, and the Red River, which is in the north, both end in the South China Sea. They spread out to very large swampy plains. These marshy lands are called deltas and they are the perfect fertile moist soil to grow rice and other crops important to Vietnam's agriculture.

WHERE DOES THE POPULATION OF VIETNAM LIVE?

Most of the people of Vietnam have their homes in the countryside. The concentration of the population is in the delta areas where farmers plant their crops.

In recent years, there has been some population influx to the major cities of Ho Chi Minh, which was formerly the city of Saigon, as well as to the city of Hanoi. The country's largest city is the city of Ho Chi Minh and a huge marble and granite tomb that pays homage to the communist leader is located there.

Ho Chi Minh City

Cao Dai Temple

RELIGION

Vietnam doesn't have an official religion. However, even though it's under communist rule, the people are allowed to worship if they wish. The religions of Confucianism, as well as Taoism and Buddhism are practiced there.

FOOD

Vietnamese food has become very popular worldwide. It is an interesting blend of Chinese, French, and Thai styles. Local seafood, rice, fresh fruits, and vegetables combine to make a unique cuisine.

Halong Bay

NATURE

Vietnam is a country that is filled with natural beauty. It has many different types of animal habitats from forests to wetlands to mountains. Its long coastline welcomes a huge number of different animal species. Over 800 bird species have been found in Vietnam. There are also 270 different types of mammals. The waterways encourage many types of reptiles and amphibians as well.

At one time, tropical forests were dense over most of the country. Unfortunately, over the last two centuries, intense logging has decreased the forest areas down to less than 20 percent. The government has begun the process of restoring these woodlands through systematic replanting.

The country is home to some very unusual animals including the majestic Indochinese tigers, the rare Saola antelopes, and critically endangered Sumatran rhinos. The government has set aside 30 national parks to protect these important species. However, their survival is still at risk because so much land has been cleared to create lumber products and to farm.

GOVERNMENT

Vietnam is a socialist republic that is ruled by the Vietnamese Communist Party.

The National Assembly selects a president. He is the head of state and is also the armed forces commander. The president appoints the prime minister who essentially runs the government.

Presidential Palace

EXPORTS

Vietnam has many commodities and products that it exports to other countries. Agricultural products include seafood, rice, and coffee. From the manufacturing sector, the Vietnamese produce machinery as well as electronics and clothing. Vietnam is the second largest producer of rice in the world after China. They are also the largest exporter of cashews worldwide.

After the Vietnam War ended in 1975, Vietnam traded with other similar communist countries, but after the U.S.S.R collapsed in 1990, it has also traded with other non-communist nations.

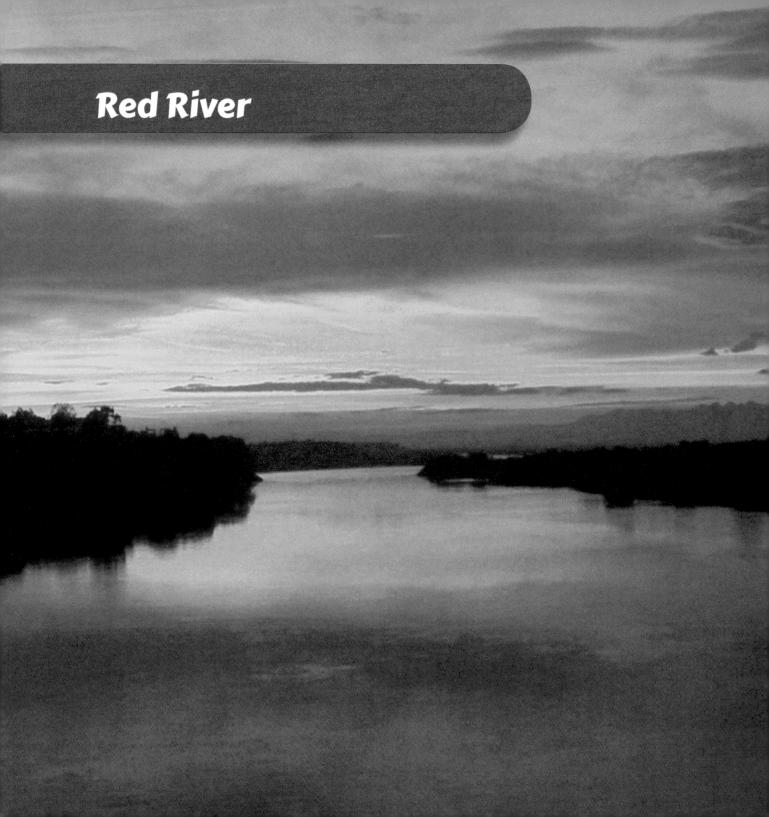

Red River

HISTORY

The very first civilizations in the country were in the valley of the Red River over 5,000 years ago. The tribes there were self-governing until a Chinese lord came in with forces and seized the country. In 207 BC, he began a kingdom that was named Nam Viet.

Ngo Quyen Mausoleum

By 111 BC, the kingdom had become absorbed into the huge empire of China. They had dominion over the land until 939 AD. At that time, a leader named Ngo Quyen, who was a Vietnamese commander, gathered the people together. They rebelled against the Chinese and drove them out. Subsequent dynasties decided to rename the country.

The new name was Dai Viet and with the new name came a takeover of land to the south. By the 1500s, there were two kingdoms that were competing against each other. Trinh was the kingdom in the north and in the south was the kingdom of Nguyen.

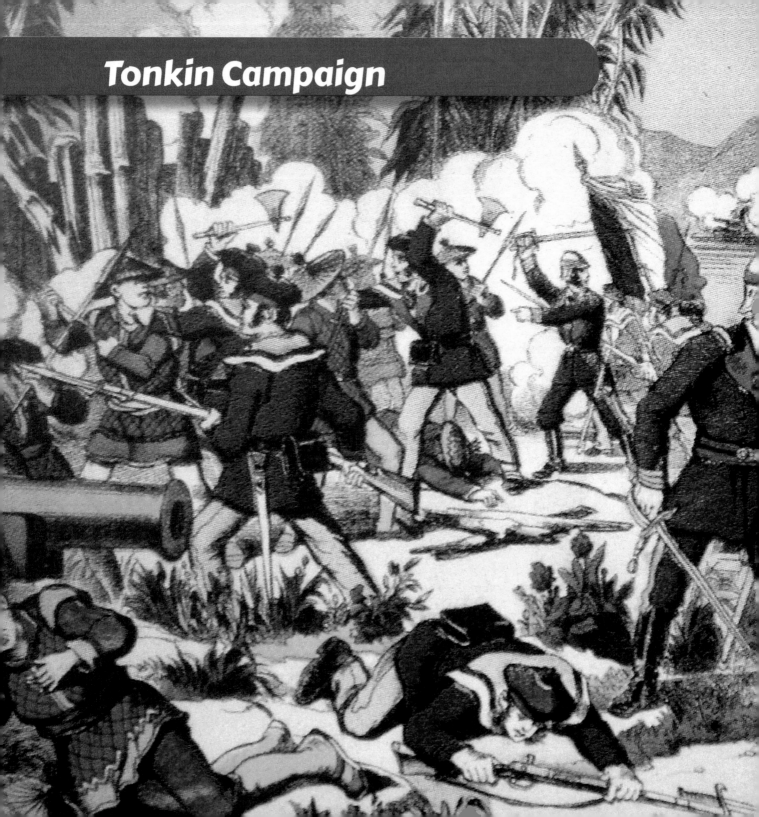

The kingdom of the south, Nguyen, had an uprising led by one of their leaders with help from France. They defeated the kingdom of Trinh. Soon thereafter the country's name was changed to Vietnam. The French were not happy with the results and decided to take the country for themselves by 1890.

Japan took control of Vietnam during the second World War, when Japan went down in defeat in 1945, the Communist leader Ho Chi Minh proclaimed Vietnam's independence. He is now hailed as an honored hero by the Vietnamese people.

Ho Chi Minh

Viet Minh Soldiers

The French tried to reclaim the land, but a war began with the Viet Minh, who were the communists in Vietnam. When the war ended in 1954, the country was divided into the north as communists and the south as non-communist.

THE BEGINNING OF THE VIETNAM WAR

Then the Viet Cong organized. This group was formed by communist rebels living in the south who wanted the south to become communist. War ensued in 1955, north against south. Then other countries made the country a battleground for the communist versus non-communist global debate.

The United States and Australia for the non-communist side and Russia, North Korea, and China for the communist side became entangled. The hot bed of fighting lasted from 1955 to 1975. The conflict became part of the Cold War.

The people of the United States were very tired of being "stuck in Vietnam." There didn't seem to be an end in sight. When Lyndon Johnson became president he decided to help the Vietnamese in the south get armed and strong enough to battle the north themselves. The US troops were held back from attacking the north, so the chance of the US winning against the communist regime was weakened.

In addition to this, the jungles of Vietnam were a very difficult place to fight. The communist troops had underground tunnels and had placed deadly booby traps everywhere. People that the US troops thought they were fighting for, attacked them.

THE END OF THE VIETNAM WAR

When Richard Nixon took office he decided to end the US entanglement in Vietnam. In 1973, he negotiated a ceasefire. A few months after this, US troops started to leave the country. South Vietnam surrendered in 1975. Vietnam was now under communist rule. The United States and its allies had lost the conflict and this loss of face had an impact during the remaining years of the Cold War.

Richard Nixon

Over 58,000 soldiers from the United States died during the Vietnam War. Being stuck in Vietnam for 20 years had cost many lives. It's estimated that millions of Vietnamese citizens and soldiers lost their lives in the war.

TODAY IN VIETNAM

Despite all that has happened, in general the people of Vietnam don't seem to harbor resentment against Americans. In fact, tourists are going to Vietnam in record numbers to experience the national beauty, culture, and ancient ruins from centuries past. There are several UNESCO World Heritage Sites in Vietnam such as Hoi, which is an ancient town with a mix of Chinese temples, French-colonial houses, and Japanese-designed bridges.

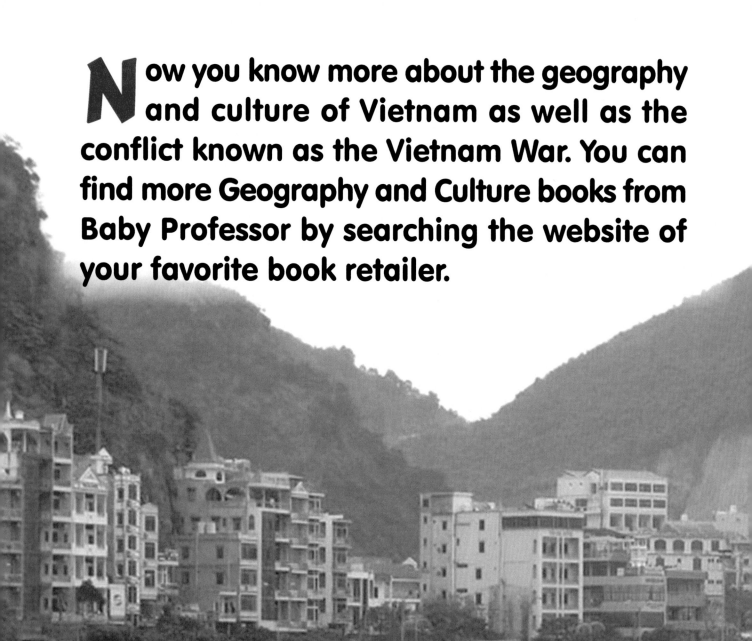

Now you know more about the geography and culture of Vietnam as well as the conflict known as the Vietnam War. You can find more Geography and Culture books from Baby Professor by searching the website of your favorite book retailer.

Visit

BABY PROFESSOR
EDUCATION KIDS

www.BabyProfessorBooks.com

to download Free Baby Professor eBooks
and view our catalog of new and exciting
Children's Books

73282356R00038

Made in the USA
San Bernardino, CA
04 April 2018